Printed in Poland
by Amazon Fulfillment
Poland Sp. z o.o., Wrocław

32883689R00074